21st Century
Junior Library

DISABILITY PRIDE

Erin Hawley

easterseals

Understanding Disability

Published in the United States of America by:

Cherry Lake Press

2395 South Huron Parkway, Suite 200, Ann Arbor, Michigan 48104
www.cherrylakepress.com

Reading Adviser: Beth Walker Gambro, MS, Ed., Reading Consultant, Yorkville, IL

Photo Credits: © Denis Kuvaev/Shutterstock.com, cover, 1, 7; © Olesia Bilkei/Shutterstock.com, 5; © Sergey Novikov/Shutterstock.com, 6, 10; © Ladanifer/Shutterstock.com, 8; © Iren_Geo/Shutterstock.com, 9; © metalmind/Shutterstock.com, 12; © a katz/Shutterstock.com, 13; © Bangkok Click Studio/Shutterstock.com, 14; © B Wright/Shutterstock.com, 17; © Jaren Jai Wicklund/Shutterstock.com, 19; © santima.studio/Shutterstock.com, 21

Cherry Lake Press is an imprint of Cherry Lake Publishing Group.

Library of Congress Cataloging-in-Publication Data
Names: Hawley, Erin, author.
Title: Disability pride / by Erin Hawley.
Description: Ann Arbor, Michigan : Cherry Lake Publishing, [2022] | Series: Understanding disability |
    Includes bibliographical references. | Audience: Grades 2-3
Identifiers: LCCN 2022005340 | ISBN 9781668909096 (hardcover) | ISBN 9781668910696 (paperback) |
    ISBN 9781668913871 (pdf) | ISBN 9781668912287 (ebook)
Subjects: LCSH: People with disabilities—Juvenile literature. | People with disabilities—Civil rights—Juvenile literature. |
    Discrimination against people with disabilities—Juvenile literature. | Respect for persons—Juvenile literature.
Classification: LCC HV1568 .H396 2022 | DDC 362.4—dc23/eng/20220210
LC record available at https://lccn.loc.gov/2022005340

Cherry Lake Press would like to acknowledge the work of the Partnership for 21st Century Learning, a Network of Battelle for Kids. Please visit http://www.battelleforkids.org/networks/p21 for more information.

Printed in the United States of America
Corporate Graphics

Easterseals is enriching education through greater disability equity, inclusion and access. Join us at www.Easterseals.com.

CONTENTS

WHAT IS DISABILITY PRIDE?

When was the last time you were proud of something you've done? Maybe it was when you had a good report card or helped someone accomplish a goal. Doesn't that **pride** feel awesome? Besides all the things you can do, you can also be proud of who you are!

People with disabilities are just like anyone else. They have hopes, dreams, friends, and goals.

I am proud of who I am!
Can you guess why?

5

People can be proud of their disabilities and proud of their identity as a disabled person. For example, you or someone you know may be **autistic**. Someone who is autistic may do things differently than someone who isn't autistic. But that difference is just a regular part of who they are. All of these differences, even beyond disability, make each person **unique**.

Autism is nothing to be ashamed or scared of.

There's no one in the world exactly alike, and there's no one in the world quite like you!

Some people view disability as something negative. This view can make people who have disabilities feel bad about themselves. It can also impact the rights of disabled people, such as access to schooling and voting.

Make a Guess!

Think about your best friend, a sibling, or parent. What is something they should be proud of?

It can make nondisabled people treat disabled people unfairly. This unfair treatment is called **ableism**.

Disability is a normal part of what makes someone unique. Disabled people have a community where they support each other and build friendships. People with disabilities do great things on their own and by working

together with others in the community. Disabled people have incredible talents, dreams, and goals. Even though a person's life may have some challenges, that doesn't mean their life or identity is bad. If people try to put down disability as a negative, let them know that disability can be something positive.

Think!

Why do you think communities are important?

Look!

With the help of an adult, do some research on the protests that helped pass the ADA. What did they look like?

THE HISTORY OF DISABILITY PRIDE AND HOW IT'S CELEBRATED TODAY

On July 26, 1990, President George H. W. Bush signed the Americans with Disabilities Act (ADA). This law gave rights to all people with disabilities. These rights include attending school, finding accessible parking, entering a building, using public transportation, and much more.

The first Disability Pride Parade took place in Boston, Massachusetts, in 1990. People with disabilities came together to not just celebrate the ADA, but to celebrate *themselves*.

Today, disability pride events take place all over the world, both in person and online. In the United States, July is Disability Pride Month. People celebrate with parades and media events. They also share pictures or videos of themselves on Instagram or TikTok using the #DisabilityPride hashtag.

Much has changed for people with disabilities, especially since the ADA law was passed. But there is still a long way to go before everyone is treated fairly.

How can you celebrate disability pride?

Advocacy is needed to make changes that help disabled people have access to more opportunities.

ADVOCACY AND PRIDE

Disability pride is not just an event. It can be a way of life. When you have pride in yourself, it is easier to deal with negativity. Even when someone has that pride, they may still have to **advocate** for themselves. Advocacy means pushing for a cause like human rights. Self-advocates are disabled people who fight for their own rights.

Many times, disabled people need help communicating or accessing different places. However, they can advocate for their own needs, wants, and rights. Self-advocacy is important because people sometimes do what they think is best for another person without truly understanding that person's needs or wants. Since everyone is different, we should listen to people with disabilities rather than assume we know what they need or want.

Create!

Think about the last time you stood up for yourself. Write down how you felt afterward. Would you change anything about what you said or did?

Listening to people with disabilities is one way to show respect.

PERSON-FIRST LANGUAGE VS. IDENTITY-FIRST LANGUAGE

Just as we should listen to people's wants, we should also listen to how people want to refer to themselves. You may have noticed the use of "person with a disability" and "disabled person" in this book. What's the difference between the two? Well, "person with a disability" is considered **person-first language**. You can tell because the word *person* comes first!

Ask Questions!

Every disabled person feels differently about what term they want to use for themselves. How could you ask someone which term they prefer?

This way of referring to someone separates the person from their disability. This action can help others see someone's **humanity** before their disability.

"Disabled person" is **identity-first language**. That's because disabled is an identity, and it comes first! This term is often preferred by those in the disability community and is becoming more common. The idea behind this language is there is nothing to be ashamed of about disability. You can't completely understand a person without seeing their disability.

EXTEND YOUR LEARNING

With the help of an adult, research three disability advocates throughout history. What were they fighting for? What did they have to say about disability pride? Choose one of these advocates and make a poster featuring their words. Use pencils, crayons, markers, paint, or anything else you want on your poster. Share your work with your family and classmates!

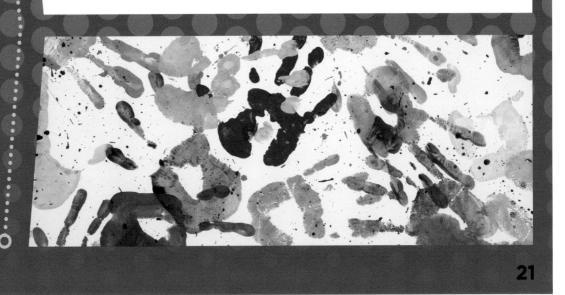

GLOSSARY

ableism (AY-buh-lih-zuhm) the unfair treatment of people with disabilities

advocate (AD-vuh-kayt) to support or argue for something

autistic (aw-TIH-stik) someone who has autism, a type of communication disability

humanity (hyoo-MAN-uh-tee) showing kindness and compassion

identity-first language (eye-DEN-tuh-tee-FUHRST LAN-gwij) putting an identity first, such as "disabled person"

person-first language (PUHR-suhn-FUHRST LAN-gwij) putting the word person first, such as "person with a disability"

pride (PRYD) being happy and confident in yourself and accepting and celebrating who you are

unique (yoo-NEEK) the only one of its type

FIND OUT MORE

Books

Bell, Cece. *El Deafo.* New York, NY: Amulet Books, 2020.

Wong, Alice, ed. *Disability Visibility: First-Person Stories from the Twenty-first Century.* New York, NY: Vintage Books, 2020.

Websites

Get Involved with Easterseals
https://www.easterseals.com/get-involved
Learn about the different ways you can get involved in increasing opportunities for people with disabilities, from advocacy to volunteering.

YouTube—TikTok Creators Show Their Disability Pride
https://youtu.be/Lc7-8xgtAvA
Three TikTok creators discuss the importance of disability representation in media.

YouTube—Wendy Lu is a Proud Disabled Woman
https://youtu.be/k2MCGqhDepY
Journalist Wendy Wu uses her voice to advocate for people with disabilities.

INDEX

ABOUT THE AUTHOR

Erin Hawley is a writer and content creator with muscular dystrophy and anxiety. Her work focuses on accessibility and disability representation in technology. She has worked with companies like Microsoft, Logitech, Adobe, and Electronic Arts to ensure that accessibility and inclusivity is not an afterthought. Erin has been featured in *The New York Times, USA Today, HuffPost*, and other publications. She lives in Keyport, New Jersey, and you can usually find her editing videos for her YouTube channel or with her nose in a book. Currently, she works as a communications and digital content producer for Easterseals National Office.